Learn How To Sew

Reuben & Sarah Doyle

Copyright © 2004-2017 by Reuben & Sarah Doyle

All rights reserved.

ISBN: 1544799063
ISBN-13: 978-1544799063

DEDICATION

This book is dedicated to those who want to learn how to sew, regardless of your age, and to those who want to teach children how to sew. May this be the beginning of a lifelong love.

CONTENTS

1	Introduction	1
2	Fundamental Sewing Skills	3
3	Threading Your Sewing Machine	9
4	Correct Needle Insertion	11
5	Installing the Bobbin	13
6	Adjustment of Tensions	17
7	The Zig Zag Stitch	21
8	Reverse Stitching	25
9	Filling The Bobbin	27
10	Making A Seam	29
11	Preparing Woven Fabrics for Cutting	33
12	The Sewing Room	35
13	Fabric/Thread/Needle Compatibles	45
14	Fabric/Thread/Needle and Stitch Length Chart	49
15	Fabric Conversion Chart	51
16	Hints For The Sewer/Crafter	53
17	8 Steps To Optimize Your Sewing Time	55
18	Sewing Projects – For The Sewing Machine	57
19	Hand Sewing – Hand Sewing Techniques	63
20	Sewing Projects – Using Hand Sewing Techniques	69
21	When Your Child Wants To Sew	77
22	Recommended Resources	79
23	Practice Pages	80

1 INTRODUCTION

Making a garment, wearing it, and having it flatter your figure gives you a wonderful sense of accomplishment. Then having someone compliment you on how nice you look, or how nice your dress or blouse looks is just the icing on the cake.

By the same token, if you're wanting to learn how to sew craft and gift items, there is no better compliment than to have someone rave over your "handmade" gift.

Anyone can learn how to sew. All you need is the "want to" – the desire to learn how to sew, and practice. A baby doesn't run a race the first time pulls himself up beside a coffee table, and a young lady doesn't automatically know how to cook just by walking into a kitchen. The same thing applies to sewing itself – it needs an operator that wants to sew and wants to be able to turn out nice gifts, craft items or clothing to wear.

If you will just take sewing one step at a time – begin by learning the various parts of the sewing machine, then how to run the sewing machine, then move on to making practice sewing projects. The same learning skills will be used when practicing the various types of hand stitches. When it's all put together, you'll be surprised at how easy and how much fun you've been having during the learning process.

This is the first day of the rest of your life – so today would be an excellent day to begin that first sewing project! Good luck with your endeavors and may you have many happy hours in the sewing room!

2 FUNDAMENTAL SEWING SKILLS

Learning to sew on a sewing machine is not hard. At the beginning you will need to learn the different parts of the sewing machine and what they do in the sewing process. Study figure 101 so you can become familiar with the various parts.

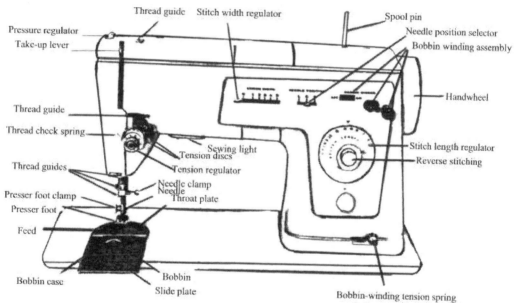

There are dozens of sewing machines on the market today, each one emphasizing what they do that other ones cannot do. In addition, there are hundreds of older models that are in homes and sewing shops all over the country. With the emphasis on the differences, it's sometimes easy to forget how basically similar all sewing machines are. All of the operating parts that are labeled on the machine on this page are common to any average machine that will do both straight and zig zag stitching. The position of some of these items may differ and be placed somewhat differently on some machines, but all the parts are there.

Lets go over the main parts that you as a sewer will need to know how to operate and adjust as you start to sew. We'll start at the lower left and work our way around the machine.

(1) BOBBIN – goes inside the bobbin case and holds the lower thread.

(2) SLIDE PLATE – is used to expose the bobbin area in order to take out the bobbin to refill, and to clean the area.
(3) BOBBIN CASE – holds the bobbin, and is located below the needle at its lowest point during its' downward stroke.
(4) FEED – is also called the "feeddog". This is the metal or rubber feed with groves or teeth, which moves the material under the presser foot.
(5) PRESSER FOOT – holds pressure on top of the fabric as the feeddog walks the material through the sewing area.
(6) PRESSER FOOT CLAMP – holds presser foot secure to the needle bar.
(7) THREAD GUIDES – guides thread inline and prevents slipping action during the sewing procedure.
(8) THREAD CHECK SPRING – maintains a small amount of pressure on the thread as the takeup lever moves up and down during the sewing action of the sewing machine.
(9) THREAD GUIDE – directs the thread in the right direction.
(10) TAKE UP LEVER – has a small hole for inserting thread as you go through the threading process. This lever raises and lowers as you sew and keeps the thread feeding correctly.
(11) PRESSURE REGULATOR – maintains pressure on the presser foot, which in turn maintains pressure on the fabric so the feeddog can walk the fabric through at a constant speed allowing the machine to make a uniform stitch on the fabric.
(12) THREAD GUIDE – guides the thread into the takeup lever hole.
(13) STITCH WIDTH REGULATOR – adjusts to determine the width of the stitch while in the zig-zag mode, or "O" adjustment for straight sewing.
(14) SPOOL PIN – holds your spool of thread during sewing operations. Some machines have two spool pins for sewing with double needles.
(15) NEEDLE POSITION SELECTOR – zig-zag machines have three positions for sewing – "left", "right" or "center", plus allows you to be able to do zig-zag sewing.
(16) BOBBIN WINDING ASSEMBLY – is used to wind the thread onto your bobbin. The machine used in the example has the assembly located at the top right, but may be located in different locations on different machines. Check your sewing machine manual for proper operation of the bobbin winding assembly.
(17) HANDWHEEL – used to move or start the sewing machine in the forward motion. If you always make your **first** stitch by turning the handwheel by hand, you will prevent the thread from being jerked down inside the bobbin area and jamming the machine.
(18) STITCH LENGTH REGULATOR – controls the length of your stitch. The stitches will be a medium length for most sewing projects. This regulator is also used when sewing in the zig-zag mode, determining whether you'll have a very closely sewn satin stitch, or wider zig zag stitch.
(19) REVERSE STITCHING – could be a knob as in the above illustration or perhaps a lever on the front side of your machine. If the reverse is a knob, it will have a "push" control in the center of the knob, and when you push it the machine will run in reverse. Or, if you have a lever, you would normally push the lever "up" to get into the reverse mode.

(20) BOBBIN WINDING TENSION SPRING – maintains pressure while winding the bobbin to insure that the thread is evenly wound.
(21) THROAT PLATE – covers and protects the bobbin area.
(22) NEEDLE – comes in assorted sizes and should be selected according to the fabric that will be used.
(23) NEEDLE CLAMP – holds the needle in place. Be sure the needle is installed correctly so the machine will work properly.
(24) TENSION REGULATOR – regulates the amount of tension on the thread check spring and is adjusted according to the weight of fabric used.
(25) TENSION DISCS – thread runs through the tension discs which have been set by the tension regulator, and gives proper tension to the thread as the machine is going through the sewing process.
(26) SEWING LIGHT – is usually placed on the underside or left side of the machine to give extra light directly in the sewing area.
(27) PRESSER FOOT LEVER – not seen from the front, as it's usually placed on the back side of the machine, and is used to lift the presser foot off the fabric in order to start or stop the sewing process, or used when turning the fabric. Look at your machine to locate the presser foot lever, and lift it up and down a time or two to see how it works.

Now that you "know" the sewing machine frontwards and backwards, it's time to do a little practice sewing.

CAUTION: Just a note of warning before you try to make the first stitch – keep your fingers away from the needle! The needle is SHARP and will definitely hurt if it goes into your finger. The proper way to sew is to guide the material (in this practice session, it will be paper) as it travels under the needle. Keep your hands away from the needle, and don't try to "push" or "pull" the fabric (paper) as it is sewing.

In order to become accustomed to actually sewing on the machine, we would like you to practice on the pre-printed designs that we have made for you. The first lesson in "sewing" will be on paper, and we want you to take all thread off the machine. Learning how to make a straight stitch, and following lines will be enough to think about, without having to deal with the thread as well. (Note: we have put extra copies of the following exercise pages in the back of the book so you can either copy them, or tear out the ones from the back to use, and still leave your book in good condition).

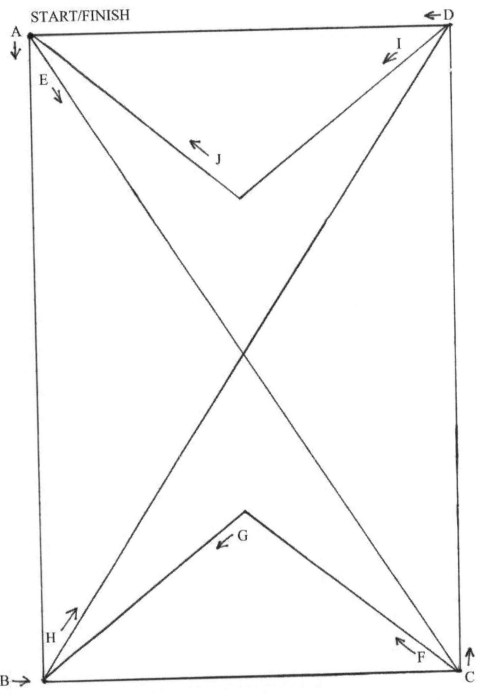

As you look over the first sewing exercise, you'll notice that we want you to learn to be comfortable making just simple straight lines. Notice the starting point is located at the top left hand corner. Starting at "A", place the beginning of the line under the needle point and let the presser foot down on the paper. Sew a straight line down to point "B", ending with the needle **in the paper**. Pick up the presser foot with your left hand and turn the paper with your right hand. Let the presser foot down and continue sewing in a straight line to point "C", then to "D", then to "E", then to "F", then to "G", then to "H", then to "I", then to "J", then back to the start/finish point.

Look over each line of needle holes that you have made. They should be on the line or very close to the line. If you've gone over the lines in quite a few places, repeat this exercise until you feel comfortable sewing in a straight line.

Try to keep a slow smooth stitching speed while sewing the straight lines. Don't try to be a speed demon with the practice sewing – just take it slow. This is where you'll learn how to get an even rhythm while sewing. Don't "speed up" for a few stitches, then slow to a stop for the next stitches, just try to keep a smooth even speed. The more you practice, the easier it will get for you.

Next put the paper with the circular design under the presser foot. Lower the presser foot and, again without thread in the machine, sew around the circles, being careful to stay on the lines. Once again, when you're finished with the circles, check the line of needle holes that you've made to check for accuracy.

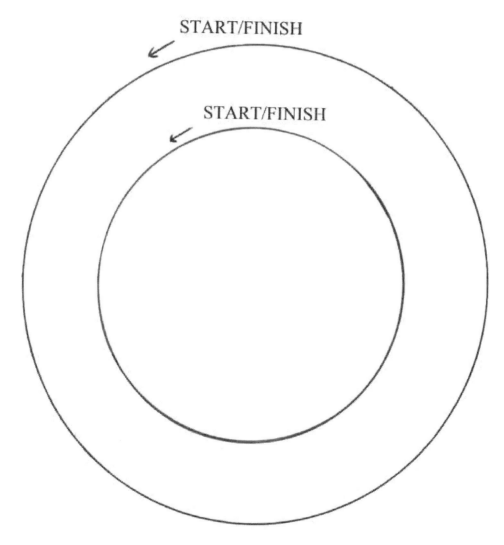

You'll notice that the "circles" are large enough that you won't be lifting and lowering the presser foot while sewing, just take it slow and turn and guide the paper with both hands while you're sewing.

The next exercise we want you to do is to make a copy of the original "straight lines" paper or use a second one from the back of this book. Use this copy to iron onto a piece of tan or white colored cotton duck fabric, or if you prefer, simply use your ruler and make similar lines on a small, "sheet of paper size" piece of the cotton duck fabric.

Before you actually can begin the practice sewing **with thread**, you must know how to thread the machine properly, how the bobbin thread works in the sewing process, and what the finished stitching should look like. The following instructions should be learned in order for you to be able to keep from having thread "jamming" problems and thread "breaking" problems with your first projects. In addition, these are things to keep in mind for all the sewing you do from this day forward.

3 THREADING YOUR SEWING MACHINE

Check your instruction manual for the correct threading of your particular machine. Basically, following the machine diagram at the beginning of the book, the steps are as follows:

1. Place the spool of thread on the spool pin.
2. Run thread across the top and around the top "thread guide".
3. Bring the thread down the front of the machine between the tension discs and around the tension regulator.
4. Next, put the thread through the "thread check spring" located behind the tension disc on the tension unit (this is the spot most beginning sewers fail to put the thread)
5. Take the thread up to the "take up lever" and thread through the hole at the end of the lever.
6. Put the thread behind the lower "thread guides", then down to the needle clamp area and you're ready to thread the needle.

4 CORRECT NEEDLE INSERTION

Locate the needle clamp on your sewing machine; this is where the needle is installed. See Figure 2A below:

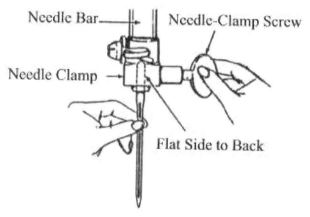

Figure 2A - Changing the Needle

It is important that you learn the proper way to insert your needle into the needle clamp. Notice that your needle will have a flat side at the upper part of the needle shaft. Notice also that there will be a "grooved" side on the needle itself, as the following illustration shows.

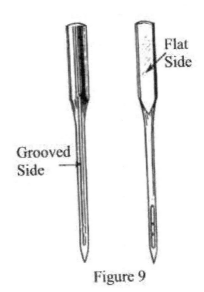

Figure 9

Raise the needle bar to the highest point, then loosen the needle clamp to remove the old needle. Place the new needle in the needle clamp with the flat side toward the back of the needle bar. The thread must lay inside the long grove of the needle as it penetrates the fabric. (Note: depending on the location of the shuttle in your specific machine, the flat side of the needle may face the right side of the needle bar instead of the back – check your machine manual to see how it has been set up by the manufacturer).

To check and make sure you have the needle inserted correctly, turn the handwheel by hand while observing as the needle enters the shuttle area, per the following diagram and instructions.

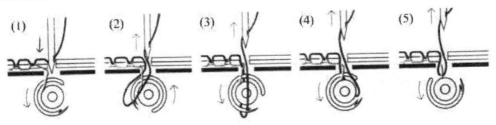

1. The needle penetrates the fabric to take the top thread into the bobbin area.
2. As the needle rises, the top thread forms a loop for the shuttle hook to catch.
3. The shuttle hook carries the thread loop around and under the bobbin case.
4. The loop slides off the hook and bobbin case, and goes around the bobbin thread.
5. The threads are pulled up and are set into the fabric as a lockstitch.

The basic requirement of all the various sewing machines is a precisely timed movement of the needle and shuttle hook to manipulate the needle thread (top thread) and the bottom thread (bobbin) to make the lockstitch.

5 INSTALLING THE BOBBIN

INSTALLING THE BOBBIN INTO THE BOBBIN CASE, and the correct way to thread the bobbin case.

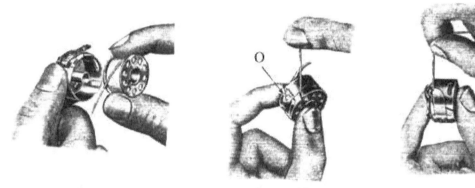

Figure F   Figure G   Figure H

1. Place the bobbin case in the left hand while holding the bobbin in your right hand, insuring that the thread end is to your left as shown in Figure F.
2. While holding the bobbin case in your left hand, insure that the slot in the bobbin case is at the top. Install the bobbin into the case as shown in Figure G.
3. Pull the thread into the slot and at the same time pull the thread under the tension spring insuring that the thread snaps under the tension spring at the very end of the spring as shown in Figure H.

CHECKING THE BOBBIN CASE FOR PROPER TENSION

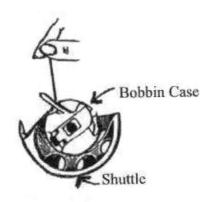

Figure I

Remove the bobbin case from the shuttle, then remove the shuttle from the shuttle carrier. Place the bobbin case, with threaded bobbin, into the shuttle, making sure that the bobbin/bobbin case has been threaded properly per instructions on Figure H. Hold the thread as shown in Figure I and shake **gently**. If the bobbin case and shuttle slide down the thread fast, you'll need to turn the adjusting screw (located on the bobbin case where the tension spring is attached) clockwise or to the right to tighten the pressure.

If the bobbin case and shuttle will not slide down the thread at all you will need to loosen the adjustment screw counter-clockwise or to the left until the bobbin and shuttle will slide down a little, but stops when you stop gently shaking the thread. At this time your tension is correct. This procedure works on nearly every sewing machine.

After you have the bobbin case tension adjusted correctly you should not have to adjust it again. You may need to make some minor adjustments to your upper tension to obtain the proper tension for the sewing machine.

CORRECT WAY TO BRING THREAD UP FROM THE BOBBIN:

The correct way of bringing the bobbin thread up after changing the bobbin is illustrated in the following diagram:

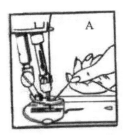 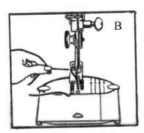 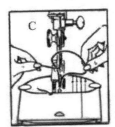 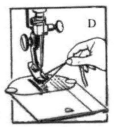

A. While holding the top thread with the left hand, turn the handwheel with the right hand until the needle is all the way down into the bobbin area.
B. Keep holding the thread and rotating the handwheel, bringing the needle up to the highest point. As the needle comes up, a loop of bobbin thread will come up with it. Pull on the top thread to draw up more of the bobbin thread.
C. Turn loose of the top thread and pull on the loop of the bobbin thread to bring up the free end of the bobbin thread.

D. Pass both the top and bobbin threads under the presser foot and take them back toward the right. Both thread ends should be at least 6" long to prevent them from being pulled into the bobbin and jamming as you begin sewing.

Always turn the hand wheel of your sewing machine **toward** you; never turn it away from you once the machine has been threaded. Also never run a threaded sewing machine unless there is a piece of fabric under the presser foot – this is probably the easiest way to jam the machine, break needles and throw the machine out of timing!

6 ADJUSTMENT OF TENSIONS

ADJUSTMENT OF UPPER TENSION

Know where the upper tension is located on your sewing machine. It can be on the front of the machine, the left side (or end) of the machine, or it could be at the top of the machine, depending on the make and manufacturer of your machine.

Before attempting to adjust the upper tension you will need to understand how the upper and lower thread works together to form a stitch and do a test to see if the tension is actually "off". (See Figure 7A, 7B and 7C)

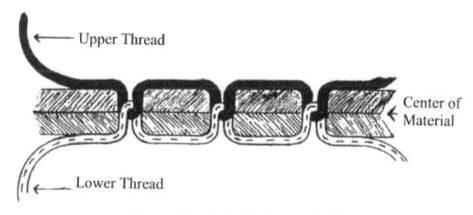

Figure 7A - CORRECT TENSION

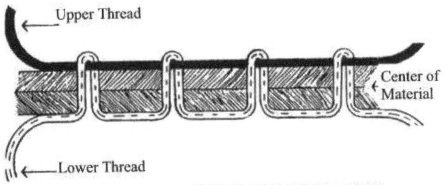

Figure 7B - UPPER TENSION TOO TIGHT

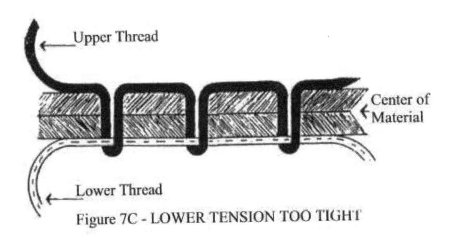

Figure 7C - LOWER TENSION TOO TIGHT

To determine whether the upper tension is too tight or too loose for the fabric you want to use, try the following test. Take a small scrap of the fabric, fold it, and stitch a line on the bias of the fabric, using different colors of thread in the bobbin and on top. Grasp the bias line of stitching between the thumb and index finger. Space the hands about 3 inches apart and pull with an even, quick force until one thread breaks. If the broken thread is the color of the thread in the needle, it means that the upper tension is too tight. If the broken thread is the color of the bobbin thread, the upper tension is too loose. If both threads break together and take more force to break it, it means that the tensions are balanced (Figure 8).

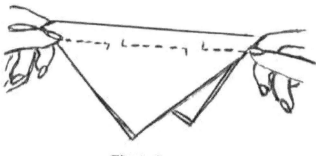

Figure 8

It is a good idea to perform the above test each time you change from a heavy to lightweight fabric, for example, changing from denim to a cotton knit or silky fabric. You'll want to be sure the tension is correct so you won't have stitching problems as soon as you start the project.

Now let's get back to the "real" sewing. To do the "straight line" practice sewing we suggest that you use a bright colored thread for the top, which will make it easy for you to tell if you're staying on the lines or very close to the lines on the cotton duck fabric.

After you've sewn enough on the straight lines that you feel comfortable with it, and are able to sew at a smooth steady speed, you can proceed to learning to sew with the machine in the "zig zag" mode.

7 THE ZIG ZAG STITCH

The "zig zag" stitch is set up using three of the controls on the front side of your machine, as shown in the following diagram. Some machines will have a "lever" and some will have a "dial" for adjusting the stitch length.

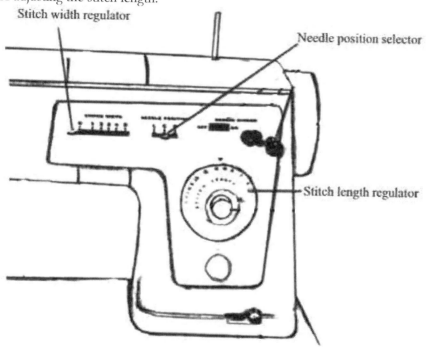

The first thing to always remember when doing any kind of zig zag stitching, is to check the "needle position selector" and make sure the needle is in the **center** position.

The "stitch **length** regulator" indicates how far apart the stitches are, and for general zig zagging, such as to finish seam edges, the position would be moved to a "mid" length position. For "satin stitch" zig zag, you would move the dial so the stitch length is very close, but not so close that the stitches would pile up in the same place. Practicing with the stitch length at various positions will show you exactly what happens in each of the positions.

The "stitch **width** regulator" is the control that determines whether you have a "wide" zig zag or just a very small width.

The following exercise will teach you how to adjust the stitch width and stitch length dials/levers in order to make the different zig zag designs. Copy the following zig zag design sheet (or take one out of the back of the book). Once again we suggest that you do the initial practice on the paper without thread in the machine; however if you're feeling brave, go ahead and iron the design onto another piece of cotton duck fabric and go to work on it – following the instructions.

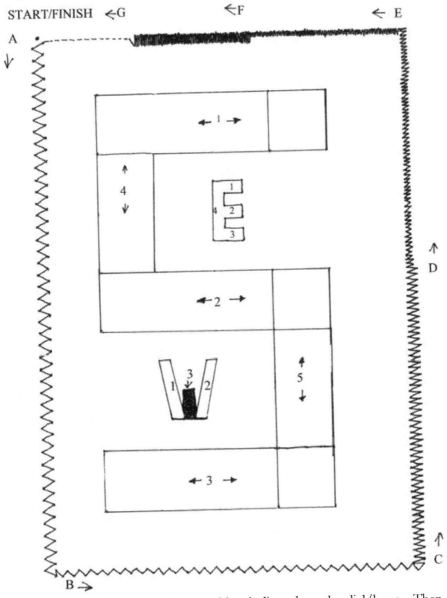

Set the stitch WIDTH to its widest position indicated on the dial/lever. Then set the stitch LENGTH dial/lever to its longest stitch position. Place the needle point at the starting point on the diagram at position "A". Sew as close as possible to the sample zig zag pattern. You will need to adjust the stitch width and length as you reach each of the "change" spots – "B", "C", "D", "E", "F", and finally back to the straight stitch at "G".

When you reach the end of pattern "A", you must stop and lift the presser foot up so you can make the 90 degree turn. After making the turn, put the presser foot down and make the adjustment to the stitch width (use the same stitch length for this line), and continue sewing to the end of the line "B".

When you reach the end of pattern "B", stop and lift the presser foot up so you can make the 90 degree turn. After making the turn, put the presser foot down and make the adjustments to the stitch width AND the stitch length. In this section, the stitch width will be at its maximum and the length just a little closer than in line "B". Sew along the line "C" until you reach "D" – again change the stitch width AND stitch length slightly to make the new stitch (the width will be closer and the length a little shorter) and sew to the end of the line "D".

When you reach the end of pattern "D", stop and lift the presser foot up so you can make the 90 degree turn. After making the turn, put the presser foot down and make the adjustments to the stitch length to make a narrow satin stitch (the width will stay about the same as section "D". For this stitch you will have the stitch length very near the end, however make sure it isn't in a "sew in one spot" stitch – you don't want the stitches to bunch up and not have the needle move forward at all. The stitches will be very close in the satin stitch.

Sew the narrow satin stitch from "E" to "F", at which point you will only change the WIDTH to a wide zig zag, leaving the stitch LENGTH as it is. The wide zig zag makes a wide satin stitch that can be used in making letters for monogramming, or embroidery and will be the stitch used if you choose to fill in the letters on the inside of this outline stitching.

When you reach "G", stop and change the dials back to a regular straight stitch – the stitch width will go to zero and make the stitch length the regular length you've been using for the straight stitching.

You may want to practice sewing in the zig zag mode until you feel comfortable with all the settings that are required in changing from one pattern to the next pattern of your choice.

On many of the later model sewing machines you will have some "built in" stitch designs on a lever or dial. Following the instructions in your sewing machine manual, you will need to set the stitch length and stitch width dials/levers as they dictate in order for the machine to make each of the designs.

In this basic "learn how to sew" book, we're only going to be using basic stitches, zig zag widths and settings that are common to every sewing machine. Regardless of what kind of machine you may have, as long as it will do zig zag (not just a "straight stitch" machine), you can make all the pretty zig zag styles that are shown on our example practice page.

If you have chosen to "fill in" the letters "S" E" W" that are inside the outline stitching just completed, you will follow the sequence indicated on the letters. Your stitch length and width will look like item "F" on the outline. Start at the top right side and zig zag all the way to the left hand corner, then start back to the right to where you started, keeping the second row of stitching close to the first row, so no white fabric shows through. Do this until you have filled in the complete block "1".

Move to block "2" and to block "3" filling them in the same way you did for block "1". Next turn your fabric sideways and fill in blocks "4" and "5" in the same way you did blocks "1", "2" and "3".

To zig zag the letter "E", adjust the stitch width to fit inside the letter. The length will stay the same, as you're still making a satin stitch, but just a little bit narrower. Again, start at "1" and zig zag across the top, then the middle bar "2", then the lower bar "3". Turn the fabric so the letter faces up and fill in the side bar "4". The reason for doing the side bar "4" last is to cover the stitches you've made in "1", "2", and "3" to give the letter a uniform look.

The letter "W" will be stitched using the same length and width that you used on the letter "E". Again start with "1", then "2", and lastly do "3".

The following drawing gives an idea of what the "picture" could look like when finished – of course you can use any color you want for the stitching, and you'll notice that we've done a wide satin stitch along the bars of the letter "S".

You may want to put this "picture" in a frame and hang it in your sewing room when you get it finished. You'll be very proud of your handiwork and will want to show it off.

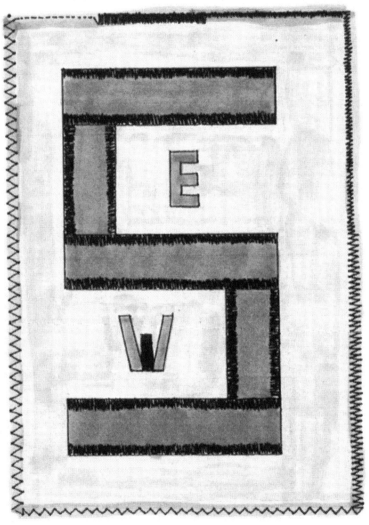

8 REVERSE STITCHING

Up to this point you've only been working with "forward" stitching, and we now want to introduce you to "reverse", and what it will be used for.

Reverse stitching

    The "reverse" could be a knob, as in the above illustration, or it could be a lever on the front side of your machine. If the reverse is a knob, it will have a "push" control in the center of the knob, and when you push the center of the knob, the machine will run in reverse. Or, if you have a lever, you would normally push the lever "up" to get into the reverse mode.

    Reverse is normally used at the beginning or ending of a seam in order to "tie" the stitches. To "tie" the stitch at the beginning of a seam, place the fabric under the needle in the position where you're going to start to sew. Find the ends of the upper and bobbin threads and pull them to the left of your work. Gently hold these ends while you make your first few stitches – by holding the ends it will keep them from being "pulled" into the bobbin area and possible jamming the machine. After sewing three or four stitches, push in the reverse button, or lift the lever into reverse, and back up two or three stitches to secure the seamline. Now continue your stitching until you get to the end of the seam. Once again, when you reach the end, put the machine in reverse and back up two or three stitches to "tie" the threads at the end of the seam. By doing this step, you'll keep the seam from starting to come apart at the end because of having loose threads there.

9 FILLING THE BOBBIN

By this time you're probably just about out of bobbin thread and wondering what to do next. Your sewing machine manual will show you where the bobbin winder is, and should give instructions on winding the bobbin.

The following diagram gives one example of where the bobbin winder unit is on a machine – yours may be located on the side of the machine, or on top of the machine, depending on what make and model of sewing machine you have, or you may have the type that rewinds right in the machine.

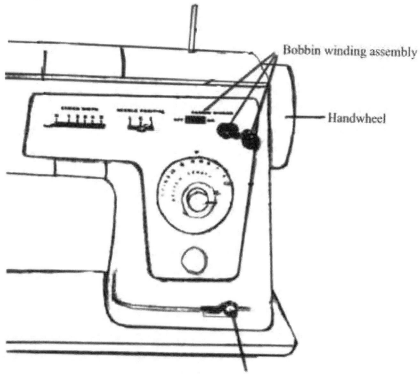

Regardless of "where" you wind the bobbin, there are some general rules that apply to every bobbin on every machine.

1. Always start with an empty bobbin. Never wind one color over another color.
2. Choose thread that is identical in color and type as the one to be used for the upper thread.
3. Wind the bobbin evenly across and in level layers. The following illustration shows the "right" and "wrong" ways to fill a bobbin:

1. Don't wind the bobbin so full that it would be tight and hard to insert into the bobbin case. Most machines have an automatic "shut off" when the bobbin gets full, but if yours does not, be careful not to fill it too full.
2. If your bobbin is slightly bent or has a nick in it, throw it away and get a new bobbin.
3. Keep the lint out of the bobbin area. Lint and broken or frayed pieces of thread accumulate in the bobbin area, and can cause problems with sewing, so be sure to keep that area cleaned out.
4. Be sure to use the RIGHT bobbin for your machine. If you've gotten some bobbins from another person, or perhaps extra bobbins from a machine you've bought, double check to make sure the bobbins are the type your machine calls for.
5. It is good to have extra bobbins on hand so you won't be tempted to put one color thread on top of another color. In addition, if you're going to be involved in a rather long project that will require a lot of thread, such as quilting, or perhaps something that will need a lot of "satin" stitching, it would be a good idea to fill 2 or 3 bobbins with the thread that you'll be using for the project, so you won't have to stop in the middle of the project and start filling bobbins.

10 MAKING A SEAM

The seam is the basic structural element of any garment and must be made with care. Although 5/8" is the standard seam width, always check your pattern or instructions for required width in special seaming situations. Seams should be backstitched at the beginning and end for reinforcement.

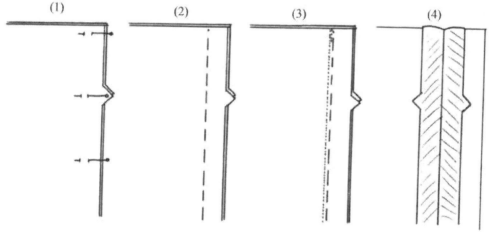

(1) Pin-baste the seam at regular intervals, matching notches and other markings. Place pins perpendicular to the seam line with tips just beyond the seam line and heads toward the seam edge. The reason for placing the pin heads toward the seam edge is so they will be easy to remove during the sewing process.

(2) Hand-baste close to the seam line, removing pins as you baste. As your skill increases, it may not always be necessary to hand baste, but simply remove the pins as you sew with the sewing machine down the seam line.

(3) Position the needle in the seam line ½" from the end and lower the presser foot. Backstitch to the end, then stitch forward on the seam line, close but not through the basting. Backstitch ½" at the end. If the seam was pin-basted, remove the pins as you stitch. Clip the threads close to the stitching.

(4) Remove the basting thread. Unless instructions specify another pressing method, the seams are first pressed flat in the same direction as they were

stitched, then pressed open. Some seams may need clipping or notching before being pressed open, such as curving seams.

There are three main types of seams that you, a beginner or less experienced sewer, will be using for most of the initial sewing items you will make.

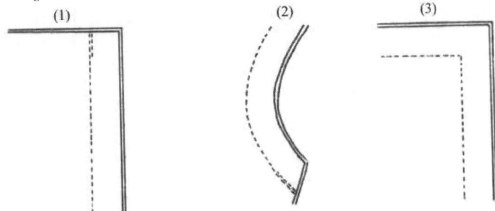

(1) **A straight seam** is the one that is used most often. In a well-made straight seam, the stitching is exactly the same distance from the seam edge the entire length of the seam. In most cases, a plain straight stitch is used. For stretchy fabrics, however, a tiny zigzag or special machine stitch may be used.

(2) **A curved seam** requires careful guiding as it passes under the needle so that the entire seam line will be the same even distance from the edge. The separate seam guide will help here, so will running the machine slower than usual.

(3) **A cornered seam** needs reinforcement at the angle to strengthen it. This is done by using small stitches for 1" on either side of the corner. After completing the "corner" you can switch back to the regular stitch length. It is also important to pivot with accuracy so the seam line will be correct on both sides of the corner.

A seam finish is any technique used to make a seam edge look neater and/or keep it from raveling. Though not essential to the completion of the craft item or garment, it can add measurably to its life. Three basic seam finishes are discussed here.

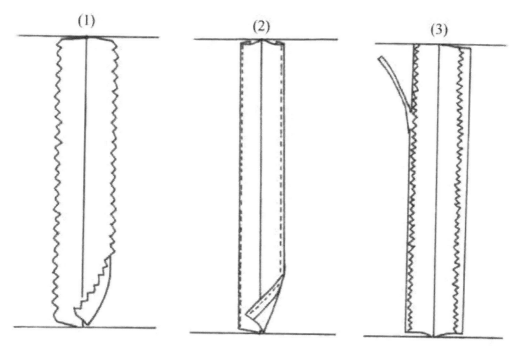

(1) **Pinked:** Cut along the edge of the seam allowance with pinking shears. For best results, do not fully open the shears nor close all the way to the points. If the fabric is crisp and lightweight, it is possible to trim two edges at once before pressing the seam open. Otherwise do one edge at a time. Pinking is attractive, but will not of itself prevent raveling.

(2) **Turned and stitched** (also called clean-finished): Turn under the edge of the seam allowance 1/8" (1/4" if the fabric ravels easily) and press. Stitch along the edge of the fold. It may be helpful, on difficult fabrics or curved edges, to place a row of stitching at the 1/8" or ¼" fold line to help turn the edge under. This is a neat, tailored finish for light to medium weight fabrics, and is suitable for an unlined jacket

(3) **Zigzagged:** Set the stitch for medium width and short (about 15) length. Then stitch near, but not on, the edge of the seam allowance. Trim close to the stitching. This is one of the quickest and most effective ways to finish a fabric that ravels. It can be used for a knit, but special care must be taken not to stretch the seam edge, or it will ripple.

11 PREPARING WOVEN FABRICS FOR CUTTING

Proper fabric preparation is an essential preliminary to cutting, and you need to understand the basic facts of fabric structure before starting any project.

Look at a piece of fabric; hold it in your hands so you can better understand the terms we're using.

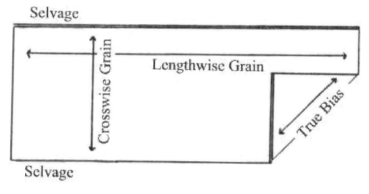

A firmly woven strip, called **selvage** is formed along each lengthwise edge of the finished fabric – it comes this way from the mill when the fabric was made.

The term **"grain"** indicates the direction of the fibers in the woven fabric – **lengthwise** or **crosswise**. The **lengthwise grain**, which parallels the finished selvage edges, is the strongest grain, and because of its strength, is the one which must always run vertically in a garment to make it hang properly. The lengthwise grain has very little give or stretch.

The **crosswise grain**, has more give and will stretch a little therefore drapes differently, giving a fuller look to a garment. Any border print type fabric will need to be cut using the "crosswise" grain.

The **true bias** grain is the diagonal edge formed when the fabric is folded so that the crosswise threads and the lengthwise threads run in the same direction. A bias-cut garment usually drapes softly, as in circular skirts, but also tends to be the cause of sagging hemlines. The true bias is very attractive when sewing plaids and checks.

Because of the uncertainty of how much woven fabrics will shrink, it is normally suggested that you run the fabric through a rinse cycle of the wash machine, then through the dryer. This will prevent shrinkage happening after you've spent hours working on a garment, then have it shrink the first time you wash it!

After running the fabric through the washer and dryer, press the fabric, ensuring that you press out the "fold line" of the fabric. If, after washing, the fold line is still very visible and doesn't want to press out, chances are it will never come out, so try to avoid using it in an area where you'll "see" the line each time the garment is worn.

12 THE SEWING ROOM

Doctors, dentists, architects and artists have special tools for special purposes, and so does the home sewer and/or the seamstress who makes a living doing sewing for others. Your work will be much easier and more satisfying when you have the needed assortment of needles, thimbles, scissors, measuring guides, hem tape, chalk, etc.

As a beginner sewer you will need a good quality sewing machine; one that will do both straight stitching as well as zigzag stitching. At this time you need not purchase an expensive sewing machine with all the bells and whistles, fancy sewing cams, etc. Keep it simple until you have become very comfortable with all the aspects of sewing, because trying to learn to sew on a machine that will do everything in the world could become so frustrating and complicated that it could cause you to give up. A good quality basic sewing machine would last you for years and allow you to do all the types of sewing, crafting, quilting that you could imagine.

Most sewing machines come with a variety of attachments – yours may have just a few attachments, or could have most of the ones we'll mention at this time. We just want you to be aware of what the attachments are and what they are used for.

SEWING MACHINE ATTACHMENTS

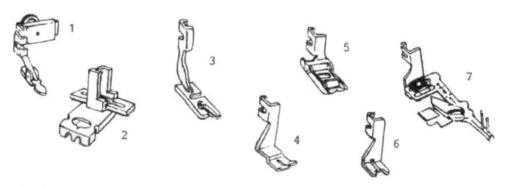

1. ZIPPER FOOT – this foot is designed so that you can stitch very close to a raised edge like a zipper, or on cording.
2. INVISIBLE ZIPPER FOOT – this foot is designed to stitch an invisible zipper. The foot is usually adaptable to both the sipper and sewing machine style by means of plastic parts (this is usually purchased separately from a notions supply department).

3. HEMMING FOOT – this foot is designed to form and stitch a perfect hem without basting or pressing in advance. It makes the small "shirt tail" type of hem. It is also used to attach ruffles, lace, or any decorative trim.
4. GATHERING FOOT – this foot is designed to lock uniform fullness into each stitch. It is to be used for shirring and gathering.
5. ROLLER FOOT – this foot is designed to feed hard-to-handle fabrics like nylon or vinyl without slipping.
6. BUTTON FOOT – this foot is designed to hold a 2 or 4-hole button firmly for zigzag or automatic stitching to secure it to the garment.
7. BINDER FOOT – this foot is designed to apply bias binding to an unfinished edge without pinning or basting in advance.

SCISSORS

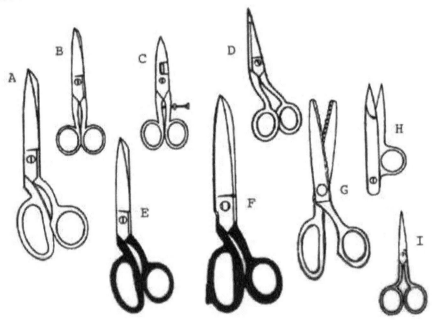

A. BENT HANDLE DRESSMAKE SHEARS are best for pattern cutting. The angle of the lower blade lets the fabric be flat. Dressmaker shears are made in 6" to 12" lengths; however the 7" and 8" are the most widely used.
B. SEWING SCISSORS are grouped in with the "miscellaneous" scissors to be used as general all-purpose sewing room cutting – come in 5" and 6" lengths.
C. BUTTONHOLE SCISSORS, just like the name, are 4 ½" long, and are used to cut buttonholes.
D. SEWING MACHINE EMBROIDERY SCISSORS make cutting and clipping easy when you're doing sewing machine embroidery.
E. HEAVY DUTY INDUSTRIAL SERRATED BENT TRIMMERS in 8" length comes in handy if you're doing sewing with denims.
F. 10" LENGTH HEAVY DUTY INDUSTRIAL SERRATED BENT TRIMMERS – same as the 8" except would be used on extra heavy fabrics such as canvas.
G. PINKING SHEARS come right and left handed, as most scissors do. These are used on fabrics that may ravel, so you can make zigzag ravel-resistant edges.

Also available are "scalloping" shears and other decorative design shears that can be used for decorative edges as well as the fancy cut note cards or photo album edges, etc.

H. THREAD CLIPS are one of the most widely used and favored scissors in the sewing room. Use them for clipping threads at the beginning and ends of seams as you're sewing, when changing colors, etc.

I. HAND EMBROIDERY SCISSORS are designed for use in hand embroidery projects.

Probably every project you work on, whether a garment or craft item, will include some hand sewing as well as machine sewing. The proper hand sewing needle is important to the overall workmanship of your project. Following is a listing of the various types of hand sewing needles and their general purpose.

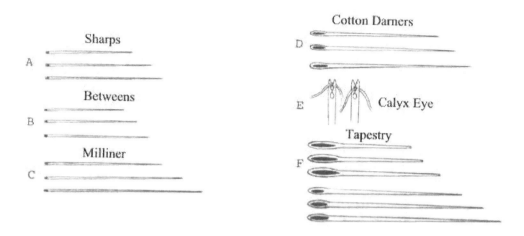

A. SHARPS (sizes 1-12) are the most commonly used hand sewing needles. They are medium length, have a round eye and are suitable for almost all fabric.

B. BETWEENS (sizes 1-12) are also known as "quilting" needles. Because they are shorter in length, using them will enable you to take fine stitches in heavy fabric.

C. MILLINERS (sizes 3/0-12) are the longer needles in the group and work very well for basting.

D. DARNERS (sizes 1-9) are designed for darning with fine cotton or wool.

E. CALYX-EYES (sizes 4-8) are similar to sharps except that the thread is pulled into a slot rather than threaded through the eye.

F. TAPESTRY needles (sizes 13-26) are heavy and have blunt points. These needles are used mainly for needlepoint and tapestry work.

Of course there are many other types of needles (long, thin beading needles, curved upholstery needles, large eyed yarn darners, medium length, long eyed crewels for embroidery, etc), but you can readily see that what we have pictured will give you a big variety for most of the projects you'll be doing.

Just as there are certain sewing machine needles designed for particular fabrics, the same thing is true with hand sewing needles. The following chart will give you the thread and needle sizes to use for various types of hand sewing.

HAND SEWING PROJECT/THREAD/NEEDLE CHART

PROJECT	THREAD TYPE	NEEDLE TYPE
Embroidery	Embroidery floss, yarn	Embroidery, sharps, yarn darner
Fastenings	Cotton, synthetic thread, silk D, button and carpet (for heavy fastenings	Embroidery, sharps, betweens
Gathering and shirring	Cotton, synthetics, elastic, Silk A	Embroidery, sharps, betweens
Quilting	Quilting or other thread, depending on the effect desired	Betweens
Top-Stitching	Cotton, synthetics, Silk A or Silk D	Betweens, sharps

Every sewing room needs to have a basic supply of sewing notions readily available in order to be able to complete whatever project you will be working on. We've mentioned the scissors and a few types of specialized hand sewing needles, and now will cover a small assortment of general sewing notions and what they're used for. You may already have some of the items in a sewing "repair" basket, or if you're just now getting into "sewing" you may need to take a trip to a sewing supply/fabric store to get stocked up on your choice of the following items. As a side note, http://SewWithSarah.com does carry most of the notions described, so you could check them out online for ordering convenience.

PINS AND NEEDLES

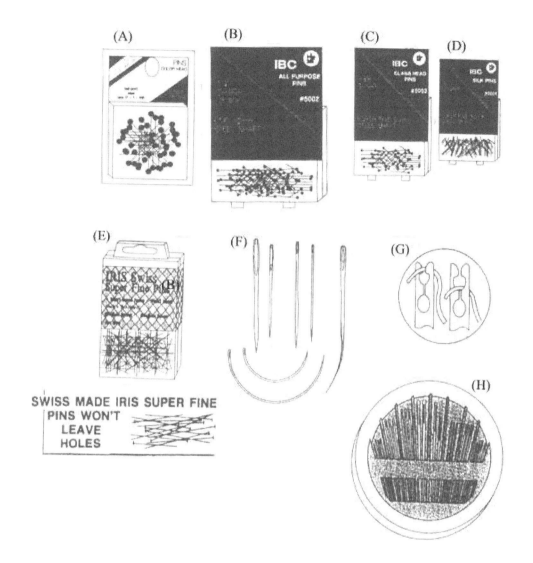

The use of proper pins for your sewing and craft projects is as important as using the right needles and thread. We will not attempt to discuss every pin on the market, but only a few of the most popular ones.

(A) IBC SILK PINS are 1 ¼" long and are super fine – finer than any other silk pin. Leaves no snags, leaves no holes.

(B) IBC GLASS HEAD PINS are 1 3/8" long and also super fine. The ultimate smooth silk pin, even longer than usual; glass head makes them easy to see.

(C) IBC ALL PURPOSE PINS are 1 ½" long, are smooth and fine. These can be used on even fine knits – weave the extra long pins into the fabric and they won't fall out. Can also be used on Ultra Suede as they won't leave holes.

(D) IBC QUILTING PINS are 1 ¾" long and fine. These are the same smooth pins as the all purpose pin only ¼" longer for bulky quilting projects. The yellow head makes them easy to see.

(E) IRIS SUPER FINE PINS are Swiss made and are extra fine. These pins are 1 ¼" long and won't leave holes and won't bend.

(F) NEEDLE REPAIR KIT contains multi-purpose straight and curved needles including carpet, mattress needles, quilting, leather and embroidery needles.

(G) EASY THREADING NEEDLES – for people having difficulty threading needles. It's as easy as lining up thread with the needle eye, give a slight pull and the needle is threaded.

(H) HOUSEHOLD ASSORTMENT needle pack contains assorted sizes of sharps, embroidery/crewels, cotton darners and yarn darner.

MEASURING TOOLS

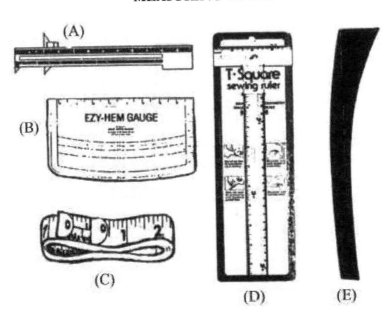

(A) SEWING GAUGE – 6" aluminum for measuring hems, checking distances between buttons, and any area that needs measuring so you won't have to dig out the yardstick.

(B) EZY-HEM GAUGE – aluminum, for pressing up hems.

(C) TAPE MEASURE – 60" in length. Most tape measures have inches on one side and centimeters on the other side. I'd recommend having two or three tape measures – they're cheap to buy, and one of the most useful items you can have.

(D) T-SQUARE – 12" ruler shaped like a T with parallel cutout slots; perfect for pattern making and adjusting commercial "store bought" patterns.

(E) CURVED RULER – used in pattern making for making hip line curves, waistline curves and armhole to waist curves. Also used in altering "store bought" patterns.

MARKING TOOLS

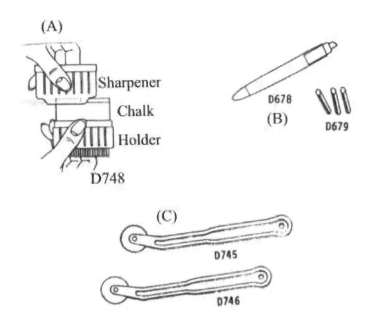

(A) TAILOR'S CHALK WITH HOLDER – plastic case keeps hands clean. Complete with white chalk, built-in chalk sharpener and brush eraser. Extra chalk can be bought separately to use in the holder.
(B) TAILOR CHALK PENCIL – holder for "pencil" type chalk for marking narrower lines than regular chalk. Comes with pencil chalk – extra chalk can be bought separately.
(C) TRACING WHEELS – D745 has a serrated wheel, which is suited for most fabrics, especially smooth, hard surface fabrics. Has a light weight, high impact handle, contoured for comfort and maneuverability. D746 has a smooth edge for firm, continuous markings. Protects pattern from tearing. This is recommended for knits and hard-to-mark fabrics.

RIPPERS/THREADERS

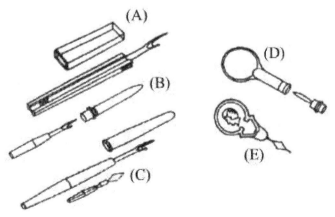

A-B-C SEAM RIPPERS come several ways. The DELUXE (A) is hardened steel with safety ball and clear cap; the COMPACT (B) is smaller for use in more delicate sewing areas, and the RIPPER/THREADER (C) has a seam ripper at one end and a needle threader at the other end.

D-E NEEDLE THREADERS also come in various styles. The needle threader WITH MAGNIFIER (D) has a wire threader. Regular threaders for hand and machine needles (E) come 3 to a package.

MISCELLANEOUS NOTIONS

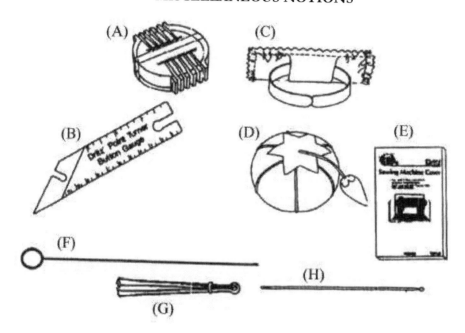

(A) BEESWAX & HOLDER – reduces static, tangling and knotting. Strengthens thread. Plastic holder keeps wax and fingers clean.

(B) POINT TURNER/BUTTON GAUGE – for pushing out corners of collars. Button gauge for making various heights of buttons.

(C) WRIST PIN CUSHION – puts the pins where you need them regardless of where you are working.

(D) TOMATO PIN CUSHION with strawberry emery – holds all your pins and needles, and you can use the strawberry emery to sharpen the pins and needles if they become dull.

(E) SEWING MACHINE COVER – a most important item to keep dust away from the machine when it's not in use. I recommend that you always keep it covered, or put away if you have a cabinet, when you won't be using it for a few days.

(F) LOOP TURNER – latch hook holds and turns bias tubing, 10" long.

(G) CLAMP TYPE BODKIN for inserting elastic, ribbon and drawstrings.

(H) ROD TYPE BODKIN with ball end for turning things inside out.

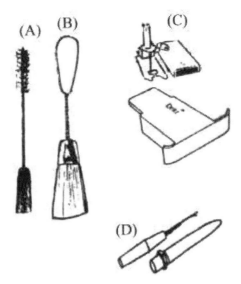

(A) LINT BRUSH with spiral brush for cleaning shuttle, tension, bobbin area, etc.
(B) LINT BRUSH without the spiral brush, but a little wider "brush" area for cleaning lint and threads away from the machine, bobbin area, etc.
(C) MAGNETIC SEAM GUIDE – fits all types of machines and insures a uniform seam width.
(D) "SNAG NAB-IT" - a small latch hook that repairs snags and pulls in knits, etc. You won't want to be without this repair tool!

13 FABRIC/THREAD/NEEDLE COMPATIBLES

The size of the needle and thread you should use depends upon the size of the fabric yarns in the fabric. The finer the yarns, the finer both the needle and thread need to be.

Needle types related to fabric structure are sharp point (regular) for woven fabrics, ball point for knits, and wedgepoint for leather and vinyl. The following illustration indicates the differences in appearance of the three types of needles:

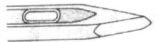

The regular sharp point needle is ideal for all woven fabrics because it helps to produce an even stitching and causes a minimum of fabric puckering. This needle is not recommended for knits, as it has a tendency to "cut" yarns and cause skipped stitches. This needle comes in a wide range of sizes from the finest size 9 to a heavy size 18. There are also the twin needle versions of the sharp point designed for fancy top stitching.

The ball point needle is specifically designed for knit and elastic fabrics. This needle pushes between the fabric yarns rather than "cutting through" the yarns. This needle comes in sizes 9 to 16. The larger the needle size, the more rounded the needle point is.

The wedge point needle, which is designed for leather and vinyl, easily pierces these fabrics to make a hole that will close back upon itself. This eliminates unattractive holes in the garment, and also reduces the risk of the stitches tearing the fabric. The wedge point needle comes in sizes 11 to 18. The size 11 needle is designed for soft pliable leathers, while size 18 is suitable for heavy or multiple layers of leather.

Thread type is chosen for its compatibility with the fabric's structure and fiber content as well as the type of project being worked on. The following chart shows the various types of thread and its usage. Where size numbers apply, the higher the number, the finer the thread – the median size is 50. Where letters indicate the size, A is fine and D is heavy.

THREAD	FIBERS AND USAGE
Basting	**Cotton:** A loosely twisted thread used for hand basting. Loose twist makes it easy to break for quick removal from

the garment. Available only in white – safest because there is no dye to rub off on the fabric.

Button and Carpet	**Cotton; Cotton-wrapped polyester:** Tough, thick thread (size 16) used for hand-sewing jobs requiring super thread strength. Thread usually has "glazed" finish that makes it easier to slip through heavy fabric.
Darning Cotton	**Cotton:** A very fine thread used for darning and mending. Strands can be separated, if desired, for work requiring even finer thread.
Elastic	**Nylon/cotton-wrapped rubber:** A thick, very stretchy thread used for shirring on sewing machines. Elastic thread should be wound on the bobbin only.
Embroidery Floss	**Cotton; rayon:** Six thread strands twisted loosely together, made for decorative hand work. Strands can be separated for very fine work.
Extra-fine	**Cotton; polyester; cotton-wrapped polyester:** Thread (approximately size 60) used for lingerie or other work requiring a fine thread.
General Purpose	**Cotton:** A medium thickness (size 50) is available in a wide range of colors (other sizes made in black and white only). Used for machine and hand sewing on light- and medium-weight cottons, rayons and linens. Cotton thread is usually mercerized, a finishing process that makes it smooth and lustrous, also helping it to take dye better. The lack of "give" in cotton thread makes it an unwise choice for knits or other stretchy fabrics, as the stitches tend to pop. **Silk:** A fine (size A), strong thread for hand and machine sewing on silk and wool. Its fineness makes it ideal for basting all fabric types, as it does not leave holes from stitching or imprints after pressing. Because of its elasticity, silk is also suitable for sewing any type of knit. Recommended for tailoring because it can be molded along with the fabric in shaped areas. **Nylon:** A fine (size A) strong thread for hand and machine sewing on light to medium-weight synthetics. Especially suited to nylon tricot.

Polyester: An all-purpose weight (approximately size 50), suitable for hand and machine sewing on most fabrics, but particularly recommended for woven synthetics; also for knits and other stretch fabrics of any fiber. Most polyester threads have a wax or silicone finish to help them slip through the fabric with a minimum of friction.

Cotton-wrapped polyester: An all-purpose weight (approximately size 50) for hand and machine sewing on knits or wovens, of synthetic or natural fibers or blends. Polyester core gives this thread strength and elasticity; cotton wrapping gives it a tough, heat-resistant surface.

Heavy Duty

Cotton; polyester; cotton-wrapped polyester: Coarse thread (approximately size 40) used where extra strength is required for hand or machine sewing of heavy vinyl, coating, or upholstery fabrics.

Metallic

Metallized synthetic: Shiny silver or gold colored thread, used for decorative stitching by hand or machine.

Quilting

Cotton: "Glazed" thread (size 40) used for hand or machine quilting.

Silk Twist

Silk: Coarse thread (size D) used for topstitching and hand-worked buttonholes, also for decorative hand sewing and sewing on buttons.

14 FABRIC/THREAD/NEEDLE AND STITCH LENGTH CHART

When put all together, the fabric type, thread size, needle size, and stitch length all play a very important part in completing the sewing or craft project properly. The following chart will help you make your choices easily when you start out on your next project.

FABRICS	THREAD SIZES	NEEDLE SIZES	STITCH LENGTH SETTING
Delicate: Net, chiffon, silk, voile Fine lace, organdy	Fine mercerized "A" silk, synthetic	9	15 to 20
Lightweight: Batiste, synthetic Sheers, paper taffeta, silk Chiffon, velvet, stretch fabric Tricot, plastic film	50 mercerized "A" silk, synthetic	11	12 to 15 (8 to 10 for Plastic)
Medium weight: Gingham, pique Chambray, poplin, wool crepe Muslin, linen, chintz, double Knit, jersey, flannel, wool Silk, fine corduroy, velveteen Satin, raw silk, wool suiting Drapery fabrics, stretch fabric	50 mercerized "A" silk 60 cotton Synthetic	14	12 to 15

Medium heavy: Denim, sail-cloth,
  Gabardine, tweed, coatings
    Heavy suiting, stretch fabric
  Drapery fabrics
	Heavy-Duty
	Mercerized
	"A" silk
	40 to 60 cotton
	Synthetic
		16	10 to 12

Heavy: Overcoatings, dungaree,
  Ticking, canvas, upholstery
  Fabrics
	Heavy-duty
	Mercerized
	24 to 50 cotton
		18	8 to 10

All weights: Decorative top Stitching	"D" silk ** buttonhole twist	18	6 to 12

**use with 50 mercerized or
"A" silk in bobbin

The advantages of using silk thread for sewing "dry cleanable" fabrics include its strength, elasticity, smooth finish and freedom from tangling. The strength and elasticity makes for longer wear and less popping of seams at points of strain.

15 FABRIC CONVERSION CHART

Because space on the pattern envelope does not permit the inclusion of ALL fabric widths, those listed are for the fabric types most suited to the design. If you plan to purchase fabric in a width that is not included, consult the conversion chart below for the approximate amount needed. (You might want to make a photocopy of this conversion chart to carry in your purse to have handy when you purchase fabric.) Fabric requirements are carefully calculated by experts to be economical yet adequate. Except when allowance must be made for special fabric, such as a plaid, or for involved alterations, there is no need to buy more than is specified.

FABRIC WIDTHS

	35-36"	39"	41"	44-45"	50"	52-54"	58-60"	66"
	1 3/4	1 1/2	1 1/2	1 3/8	1 1/4	1 1/8	1	7/8
	2	1 3/4	1 3/4	1 5/8	1 1/2	1 3/8	1 1/4	1 1/8
Y	2 1/4	2	2	1 3/4	1 5/8	1 1/2	1 3/8	1 1/4
A	2 1/2	2 1/4	2 1/4	2 1/8	1 3/4	1 3/4	1 5/8	1 1/2
R	2 7/8	2 1/2	2 1/2	2 1/4	2	1 7/8	1 3/4	1 5/8
D	3 1/8	2 3/4	2 3/4	2 1/2	2 1/4	2	1 7/8	1 3/4
A	3 3/8	3	2 7/8	2 3/4	2 3/8	2 1/4	2	1 7/8
G	3 3/4	3 1/4	3 1/8	2 7/8	2 5/8	2 3/8	2 1/4	2 1/8
E	4 1/4	3 1/2	3 3/8	3 1/8	2 3/4	2 5/8	2 3/8	2 1/4
	4 1/2	3 3/4	3 5/8	3 3/8	3	2 3/4	2 5/8	2 1/2
	4 3/4	4	3 7/8	3 5/8	3 1/4	2 7/8	2 3/4	2 5/8
	5	4 1/4	4 1/8	3 7/8	3 3/8	3 1/8	2 7/8	2 3/4

Add additional ¼ yard for: large difference in fabric widths, one-directional fabrics, or styles with sleeves cut in one piece with the body of the garment.

EXAMPLE: If you found some very nice fabric that you want to use for a specific pattern – the fabric is 60" wide and the pattern yardages only go up to 45" wide on the pattern package, you could be purchasing too much fabric unless you consult this conversion chart. If the pattern package says you need 1 ¾ yards of 36" wide fabric you can readily see that if you have 60" wide fabric, you'd need only 1 yard.

16 HINTS FOR THE SEWER/CRAFTER

It's much easier to work on a project when all the necessary "tools" are handy – get all the scissors, needles, pins, tape measure, etc out before beginning the project so you won't have to jump up and down to get the items once you've begun the project.

Always turn the hand wheel of your sewing machine toward you, never turn it away from you once the machine has been threaded. Also never run a threaded sewing machine unless there is a piece of fabric under the presser foot – this is probably the easiest way to jam the machine, break needles and throw the machine out of timing!

Before beginning to sew, lay both threads under and toward the back of the presser foot. The correct way of bringing the bobbin thread up after changing the bobbin is illustrated in the following diagram:

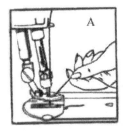 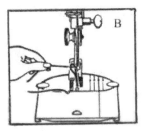 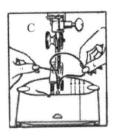 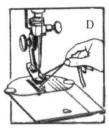

A. While holding the top thread with the left hand, turn the handwheel with the right hand until the needle is all the way down into the bobbin area.
B. Keep holding the thread and rotating the handwheel, bringing the needle up to the highest point. As the needle comes up, a loop of bobbin thread will come up with it. Pull on the top thread to draw up more of the bobbin thread.
C. Turn loose of the top thread and pull on the loop of the bobbin thread to bring up the free end of the bobbin thread.
D. Pass both the top and bobbin threads under the presser foot and take them back toward the right. Both thread ends should be at least 4" long to prevent them from being pulled into the bobbin and jamming as you begin sewing.

When beginning or ending a seam, make sure the take-up lever is in its highest position. Put a drop of oil into the hook/shuttle area regularly.

Be sure that the needle is in the center position when straight stitching. Never straight stitch with the needle in the left or right positions (an exception to this is when using a zipper foot).

It will save a great deal of "total working time" on a project if you will take care of the thread ends as each bit of stitching is completed. If you fail to do this, it will take extra time when the project is finished to trace out each loose hanging piece of thread in order to clip it. If you just leave the loose pieces of thread hanging, it will detract from the over professional look of the garment.

In some types of fabric, such as chiffon, you may find the needle will drag the fabric down into the needle hole when you begin to sew. Make sure you are using a fine needle, have the tensions set properly, and if the problem still exists, place a piece of gummed tape over the needle hole in the throat plate of the machine.

Back-stitching at the end of a line of machine stitching firmly fastens the end, but sometimes can cause puckering of the fabric. To prevent this, hold the fabric taut as you continue to operate the machine, taking several stitches in the same spot in the fabric. These several stitches will secure the thread, but use your own judgment in using this method, as you could cause damage to very fine lightweight fabrics.

Hinged presser feet on sewing machines require different handling from rigid ones because the pressure of the foot is less evenly distributed throughout its entire length. The threads have a tendency to tangle at the beginning of the stitching and the machine may stall on the tangled threads. Hold the loose thread ends gently with the right hand as you begin stitching. If the threads are slightly taut, they cannot tangle or be pulled down into the bobbin area to cause a jam.

To protect your sewing machine while it is not in use, you should place a piece of fabric under the presser foot and lower the foot onto it. Also be sure to cover the machine, as any dust settling in and around the moving parts can cause sewing problems later on.

Never oil your sewing machine without first cleaning it as well as you can, removing all the dust, lint and pieces of thread from the bobbin area and throat plate area.

There are three main points to be aware of each time the sewing machine is used: 1) Make sure the take-up lever is at its highest point when stitching is started and when the work is being removed from the machine. 2) Always drop the presser foot before changing the tension on the upper thread (if the presser foot is in the up position, you can turn the dial all day long, and the tension won't change, as it will be in the "disengaged" position). 3) When winding the bobbin, always thread the loose end of the thread through the hole in the side of the bobbin. If this loose thread end is held firmly, it will break off, leaving a smoothly wound supply of thread in your bobbin.

The selection of your thread should be based on the type of fabric you are using. The thread should blend with the fabric in color, fiber and size – refer to the previous fabric/thread/needle compatibles chart for assistance.

The selection of your needle is very important. The needle should be fine enough to prevent the fabric from being marred with large puncture holes, but still be heavy enough to pierce the fabric without bending. Remember also that the eye of the needle must be big enough for the thread to pass through freely; too fine a needle will cause the thread to fray (Refer to the fabric/thread/needle/stitch length chart previously mentioned).

17 8 STEPS TO OPTIMIZE YOUR SEWING TIME

1. Be prepared

Gather and purchase all of the supplies necessary to complete your sewing or craft project ahead of time. Having to stop in the middle of the project in order to run out and get a forgotten essential item is time consuming and irritating.

2. Check the threading of your sewing machine

Double check the threading of your sewing machine to prevent immediate stitching problems. Breaking thread or skipped stitches right off the bat can cause you to lose interest in the project, not to mention the time lost in fixing the problem. And speaking of thread, always use a good quality thread. "Cheap" thread will fray, break and cause knotting of the thread while sewing.

3. Use the correct needles for the project

It is a mistake to simply use the same needle for everything you sew until it breaks. Some fabrics require a fine needle while heavier duck type or denim fabrics require a heavier needle. Keep a supply of assorted machine needles handy so you'll have the correct needle for the fabric you'll be using. In addition, if you hit a pin, you should immediately change the needle. A bent needle, even if only "slightly" bent or nicked can cause skipped stitches and can quite possibly cause damage to your fabric.

4. Cut the fabric carefully

All pattern pieces have grainline markings. The grainline should run parallel with the length of the fabric. If you simply lay the pattern pieces anywhere on the fabric, ignoring the grainlines, the finished garment will not hang right. The extra few minutes spent laying the pattern pieces correctly and cutting the seam lines precisely will result in a professional looking garment you will be proud of.

5. Practice unusual or new techniques

If your project or garment includes a technique you are not familiar with, or haven't done in quite some time, such as buttonholes or flat felled seams, practice on a piece of extra fabric. It would be best to make two or three practice samples before actually sewing on the garment itself.

6. Clip all threads as you sew

It only takes a second to clip the stitches from the beginning and end of the seams. If you wait until the garment is finished it will become a chore and you may be tempted to leave them, resulting in an unprofessional looking garment. Be sure to have a waste basket handy, or tape a small lunch bag to the side of your sewing machine table in which to toss the threads after clipping.

7. Press seams as you work

Pressing the seams during the sewing process will produce a more professional looking garment, and will also make it easier to sew the seams that will "cross" any of the seams already sewn. Gently open the seams and press flat. You will save time if you sew several seams, then press them all at once, before moving on to the next step.

8. Clean the sewing area

Clean up the sewing area after each project. A great motto for your sewing/craft area is "a place for everything and everything in its' place". Put things away - left over fabric in a scrap box or drawer, scissors, pins and thread back in the drawer. The sewing room will look much better and an organized sewing area is much more inviting than a messy, piled up area with only a "path" to the sewing machine.

18 SEWING PROJECTS – FOR THE SEWING MACHINE

To give you some extra practice with your sewing skills, we're including a variety of sewing projects that you may use. The projects are designed so that you would be able to make some for gifts, for children that you know, as well as for you to use in your own home.

MULTI-POCKET WALL HANGING

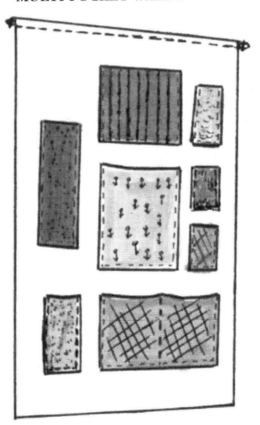

A multi-pocket organizer can be made from a bath towel or any sturdy fabric such as sport denim, sailcloth, upholstery fabric, drapery fabric, or cotton duck fabric. Cut the fabric into a 25" x 40" piece. Sew a ½" hem on the sides. Turn under 1 ½" at the top and bottom for casings and sew. Cut various sized and colored pockets made from scraps of printed or solid fabric. Turn under and sew a ¼" hem at the top of each "pocket". Next, fold under ¼" seams along the sides and bottom and press (this makes it much easier to attach the pockets). Arrange the assorted size pockets as desired on the backing and sew in place.

Insert rods at the top and bottom and hang on the wall near a play area, keeping the organizer low enough that your child can "fill" the pockets with small toys, blocks, small stuffed animals, books, etc.

The multi-pocket organizer can also be attached to a ¼" plywood backing, and attached to the wall or on the side of a dresser, etc. Children will play for hours filling the pockets, then taking everything out, then filling them again. You may want to put a multi-pocket organizer on the wall in your sewing room in an area that your small child can play safely – give them an empty round pin cushion, fabric pieces, etc in addition to some of their own toys that they can stuff into the pockets.

FISH BEAN BAG

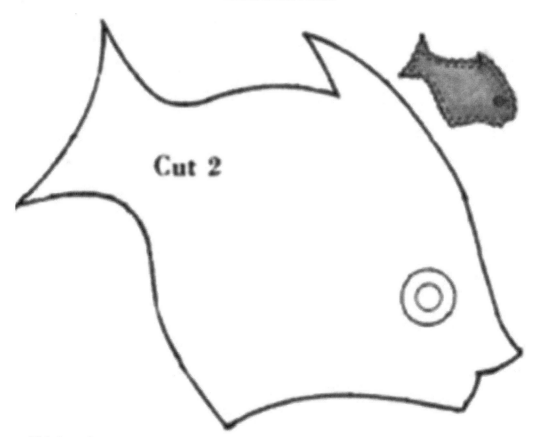

Fish bean bags are an easy sewing project for children, or for adults to make as toys for their children. Make several of them for the children to use for "bean bag toss" or any number of "bean bag" games.

Materials Needed:

Scraps of Upholstery material, terry cloth, cotton fabric, corduroy or felt

Thread to match

Buttons for eyes, or small circles of felt

Polyester Stuffing, or beans for a "real" bean bag

Pin the pattern piece on doubled cloth (need two pieces). Cut around the pattern adding a ¼" seam allowance all around.

Sew buttons in position for eyes on each piece. Pin pattern pieces together, wrong side OUT, and sew leaving an opening in order to turn right side out. Clip the corners and turn. Stuff with polyester stuffing or fill with beans. Stitch the opening closed.

TOOTH PILLOW

The "Tooth Fairy Pillow" will delight any youngster that has a loose tooth. They'll probably carry around the tooth fairy pillow hoping the tooth will fall out at any moment!

MATERIALS NEEDED:

Scraps of satin fabric

24" length of lace edging

Small amount of polyester fiberfill

Appropriate thread

Cut two 5" square of satin fabric for the pillow. Cut one small 2" x 3" pocket from a coordinating color satin fabric.

With a magic marker or pen, write the word "tooth" on the small pocket, and sew it to the center of one of the larger pieces of satin fabric, using a satin stitch on your sewing machine, leaving one of the 3" sides open to put the tooth in. (This makes a large enough opening that the tooth fairy can exchange the tooth for the money!)

Sew the two pillow pieces together with a satin stitch zig zag or ¼" seam, leaving one side open for stuffing. Turn inside out. Lightly stuff the pillow with the fiberfill, and stitch up the opening. Sew the lace to the outside edges as shown.

As an additional "personal" effect, you could also write the child's name on the pocket.

GOLF MITTENS

Golf mittens are sure to be a hit for anyone who golfs. The golf club heads are protected, and the golfer can see at a glance which club he's reaching for since you're going to conveniently put the numbers on the mittens for him.

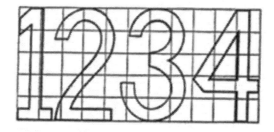

Enlarge the above numbers using the scale of each square = ½ inch.

Materials needed:

    8 pieces of felt 4 ½" x 10"

    4 felt "tabs" 3" x 3/8" wide

    Contrasting felt for numbers

    8" length of ¼" wide elastic

    22" length of plastic lacing or shoe lace

Trim the edges of the felt with pinking shears. Cut the tops of the mittens on a curve as indicated in the picture in order to fit over the golf club heads.

Enlarge the numbers above, trace and cut out of contrasting colored felt. Machine stitch each number to one side of the mitts, stitching about 1/8" IN from the edge.

Divide the 8" length of elastic into four 2-inch pieces. Sew one piece across the back of each mitt about 4 ½" up from the bottom. Stitch in the center and on each end of the elastic pieces. The elastic makes the mitten gather and holds it in place on the club.

Take the 4 felt tabs and insert the ends of the tabs into the tops of the mittens and pin in place. Stitch the front and back sides of the mittens together.

Using the 22" length of plastic lacing or shoe lace, tie the four mittens together to complete the set.

QUICK PINKED PLACEMATS

Materials Needed:

1 ¼ Yds printed fabric

2/3 Yd co-ordinating solid fabric

1 ¼ Yd Wonder Under

Appropriate Thread

Cut 4 12" x 6" and 4 10" x 14" rectangles from the printed fabric (Fig. A). Cut 4 11" x 15" rectangles from the solid color fabric (Fig. B).

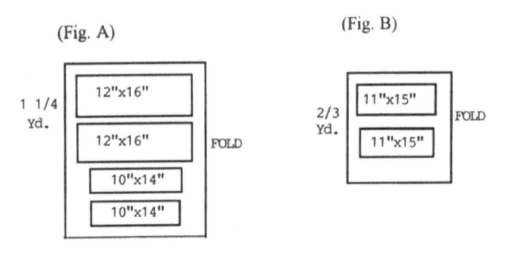

Cut 4 medium (11" x 15") and 4 small (10" x 14") rectangles from the Wonder Under and press them to the underside of the appropriate rectangles.

Place the medium rectangles on top of the large rectangles and pin the edges. Place the small rectangles on top of the medium rectangles and pin the edges. Using a warm iron, press all layers together to secure them.

For additional decorations, you can use a decorative machine stitch and satin stitch several rows around the inside of the small rectangle, making the stitching lines 1" to 1 ½" apart.

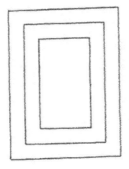 

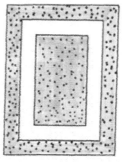

As a variation, you may want to purchase the longer length of fabric in a solid color and the smaller length in a coordinating print, then use the solid for the large and small rectangles and the print for the medium rectangle. By using this method, your fancy decorative stitching will show up much clearer.

Another variation would be to place a thin layer of polyester batting between the layers of rectangles and stitch them in place, making a "puff" placemat. In order to complete the "puff" it will be necessary to use a wide satin stitch around the medium and small rectangles to secure them in place.

Personalized placemats would be treasured by everyone who receives one, and are very easy to make. Cut a 10" x 16" piece of felt, then glue yarn or other trim in letter shapes to form the desired name. Next, using your pinking shears, cut six 2 ½" printed fabric squares and glue in place, as indicated in the diagram above. Cut a 12" x 18" piece of transparent backing material and remove the backing. Center the felt on the adhesive surface. Place rickrack all around the placemat to overlap the felt. Cut a second piece of transparent backing and remove the backing. Place the adhesive side on top of the finished placemat and seal the edges. The personalized placemats are now waterproof and cleanable.

19 HAND SEWING

All of the projects in this section can easily be made without a sewing machine. All you need is a hand sewing needle and thread color to match the fabric of the project you'll be working on.

To begin, we'll show you how to thread the needle so you'll be ready to start sewing. Next we'll give you illustrations of several basic hand sewing stitches and instructions on how to make them and where they're used.

Cut a length of thread from the spool that measures approximately 20". If the thread twists or knots as you sew, let the thread dangle with the needle end down. Carefully slide your fingers down the thread and you will feel it untwist.

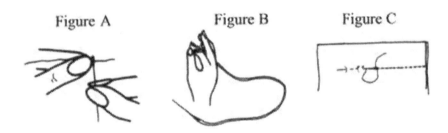

(A) Insert one end of the thread through the eye of the needle.
(B) Bring the ends of the thread together and tie into a knot as close to the end as possible.
(C) You're now ready to begin sewing. Bring the needle up through the fabric – the knot will stop the thread from coming all the way through. To sew, you'll "weave" the needle in and out of the fabric three or four times, then grab the needle gently and pull until the thread lays smooth on the fabric. Do not pull the stitches too tight nor leave them too loose. When finishing the hand sewn seam, make several stitches in one place to secure the stitching

HAND SEWING TECHNIQUES

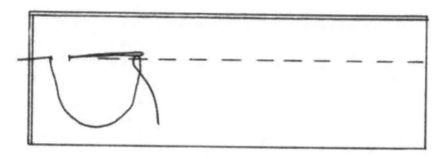

BACKSTITCH is one of the strongest and most versatile of the hand stitches. It serves to secure hand stitching and repair seams. As a beginning or end in hand stitching, bring the needle and thread to the underside. Insert the needle through all fabric layers a stitch length **behind** and bring it up just in **back** of the point where the thread emerges. Pull the thread through.

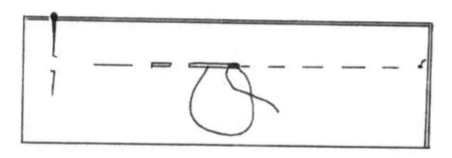

BASTING: Hand basting is used to temporarily hold together two or more fabric layers during fitting and construction. **Even basting** is used in areas that require close control, such as curved seams, seams with ease, and set-in sleeves. Short (about ¼") temporary stitches are taken the **same distance** apart. Working from right to left, take several evenly spaced stitches onto the needle before pulling it through.

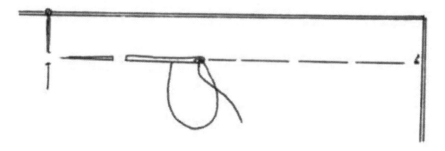

UNEVEN BASTING is used for general basting and for marking. Like even basting, these are short temporary stitches, about ¼" long, but taken about 1 inch apart.

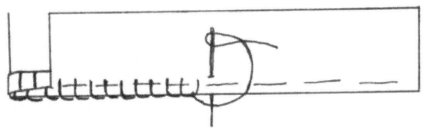

BLANKET STITCH. Traditionally an embroidery stitch, it can be used to cover fabric edges decoratively. Work from left to right, with the point of the needle and the edge of the work toward you. The edge of the fabric can be folded under or left raw. Secure the tread and bring out below the edge. For the first and each succeeding stitch, insert the needle through the fabric from right side and bring out at the edge. Keeping the thread from the previous stitch **under** the point of the needle, draw the needle and thread through, forming the stitch over the edge. Stitch size and spacing can be the same or varied.

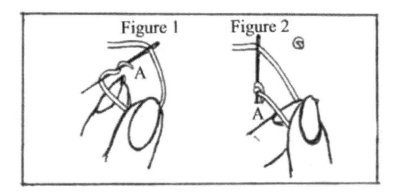

FRENCH KNOT is actually an embroidery stitch that has many applications for decorative stitching on clothing items or craft items. Bring the needle up through the material (A), wrap the thread around the tip of the needle three to five times (depending on how big a knot you want) – Figure 1. Insert the needle back into the fabric one or two threads away from where it was brought up – Figure 2. Draw the thread through carefully to form the knot on the right side. Bring the needle back up in position for the next "knot". If you look at the tiny "knot" right below the "2" in the drawing, you'll see how the finished knot will look.

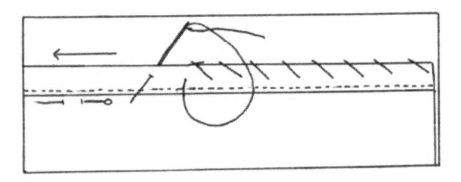

HEMMING STITCHES are used to secure a hem edge to a garment. The **slant hemming stitch** is the quickest, but least durable because so much thread is exposed and subject to abrasion. Fasten the thread on the wrong side of the hem, bringing the needle and thread through the hem edge. Working from right to left, take the first and each succeeding stitch approximately ¼" to 3/8" to the left, catching only one yarn of the garment fabric and bringing the needle up through the edge of the hem.

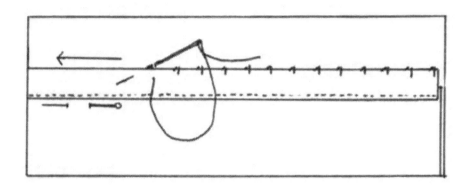

VERTICAL HEMMING STITCH is a durable and stable stitch best suited for hems whose edges are finished with seam tape. Stitches are worked from right to left. Fasten the thread from the wrong side of the hem and bring the needle and thread through the hem edge. Directly **opposite** this point and beside the hem edge, begin first and each succeeding stitch by catching only one yarn of the garment fabric. Next direct the needle down diagonally to go through the hem edge approximately ¼" to 3/8" to the left. Short, vertical stitches will show on the hem.

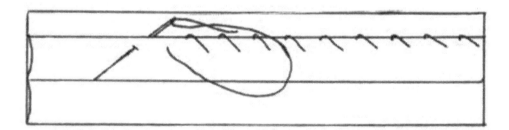

OVERCAST STITCH. This is the usual hand stitch used for finishing raw edges of fabric to prevent them from raveling. The more the fabric ravels, the deeper and closer together the overcast stitches should be. The stitches can also be used as a decorative stitch on hand sewing items. Working from either direction, take diagonal stitches over the edge, spacing them an even distance apart at a uniform depth.

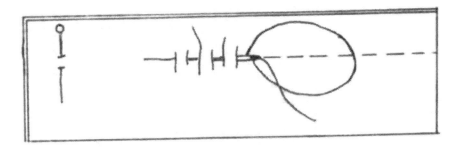

RUNNING STITCH is a very short, even stitch used for fine seaming, tucking, mending, gathering and other delicate sewing. The running stitch is like even basting except that the stitches are smaller and usually permanent. Working from right to left, weave the point of the needle in and out of the fabric several times before pulling the thread through. Keep stitches and spaces between them small and even.

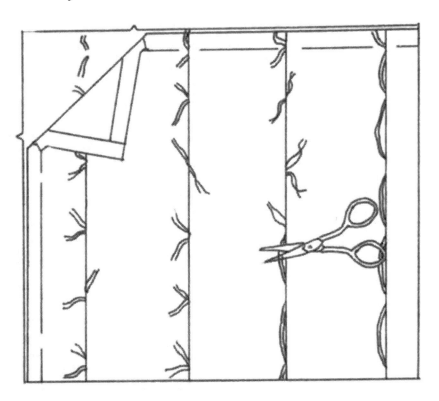

SIMPLIFIED TAILOR'S TACKS are used to transfer construction details, such as darts) and matching points from the pattern to cut fabric sections. They are basically uneven basting stitches. Using a long length of double, unknotted thread of a contrasting color than the fabric, take a small stitch on the pattern line through the pattern and fabric. Pull the needle and thread through, leaving a 1" thread end. Take similar stitches about every 2" to 3", leaving the thread slack in between. Cut the threads at the center points between stitches, as indicated in the drawing, and gently lift the pattern off the fabric, taking care **not** to pull out the thread markings.

20 SEWING PROJECTS – USING HAND SEWING TECHNIQUES

This section deals with projects that can be hand sewn, and will give you some practice on the techniques of hand sewing. The more you practice the various stitches, the more confident you will become.

COIN PURSE

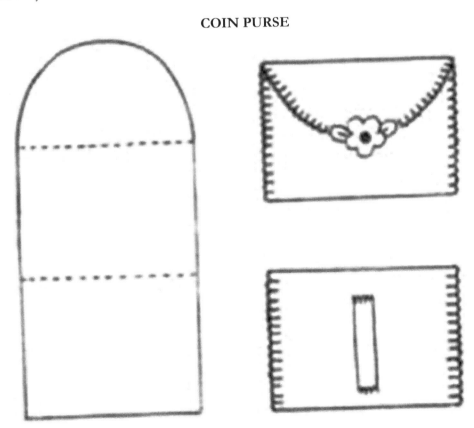

A coin purse is a very easy hand sewing project and something that would be useful for yourself, or to give as a gift.

Materials Needed:

1 10 x 12 or 9 x 12 piece of felt (your choice of color)

Felt scraps for trim

Co-ordinating color of yarn

1 snap

    Cut a pattern for the coin purse from the diagram shown above. If you'd like the coin purse to be a little bigger or smaller, you can use a photocopy machine to make the pattern larger or smaller. Pin the pattern to the felt and cut out the purse. Fold the felt along the dotted lines as shown.
    With the yarn, blanket stitch the sides together, being sure to take close, even stitches so it will hold together well. Next use the blanket stitch around the flap.
    Sew the snap in place the under side of the flap and to the purse. Cut a small flower and leaves or other design from the scraps of felt and carefully stitch them in place on top of the snap.
    If you'd like, you can stitch a small strip of felt to the back of the purse as shown, to form a handle.

BABY BLOCKS

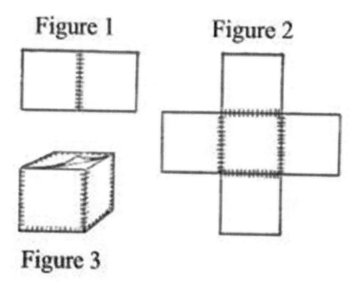

    Soft, fabric washable baby blocks have no sharp corners to hurt the baby and can be used in many ways. You can use cotton duck fabric, or upholstery fabric or "oil" cloth, which similar to what table cloths are made out of.

Materials Needed:

    ¼ Yd each of 6 colors of fabric

    1 Skein variegated yarn

Poly fiberfill stuffing

Using a yardstick, measure the fabric pieces into 3" strips and cut the strips. Next divide the strips into 3" squares, and cut. (Since each block takes only 6 squares, you'll have enough blocks to make several "sets" of blocks.

(1) Using the blanket stitch, stitch two of the blocks together, making the stitches close together.
(2) Use one of the sewn squares as a "center" square or bottom of the block, then stitch three more squares on the other sides to form a cross.
(3) Bring each of the "sides" up and stitch the edges to form the outside of the block. The last fabric square will be attached at the top to complete the block. Stitch along two sides, leaving two seams open in order to stuff the block. Stuff the block firmly with the poly fiberfill then stitch the other two sides closed, and fasten the yarn securely so it will not come unstitched.

The blocks could be made with embroidered designs on some squares and numbers on other squares. In addition, a complete set of "alphabet" blocks could be made. A "set" of blocks could be six to the set, or ten or twelve, or as mentioned previously, a complete set of 26 blocks for the alphabet.

ELEPHANT BOOKMARK

Elephant bookmarkers are easy and very inexpensive to make. Children and adults alike will appreciate the gift you've made for them.

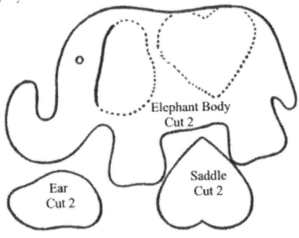

Bookmark Pattern

Materials Needed:

Scraps of two colors of felt

12-13 inch piece of ¾ inch grosgrain ribbon

Small bone or plastic ring

2 tiny beads for eyes

Small amount of cotton batting

Crochet weight cotton thread to match

Cut out the felt pieces according to the chart above – two each of the elephant body, ears and saddle. Make the saddle pieces of a contrasting color.

Overcast around the ears and stitch to each side of the head, in the position shown in the sketch. Sew a bead on each side for the eyes. With overcast stitches, sew the two body sections together, stuffing as you go with the cotton batting.

Hinge the two heart-shaped saddle sections together at the top with a few stitches, then tack to the top of the elephant back as a saddle. Pull the end of the ribbon through the center of the saddle and tack underneath the saddle to the body.

Pull the top end of the ribbon through the ring, and fasten on the wrong side with a few stitches. Your finished elephant book mark will look like the illustration on the following page.

BUTTERFLY PINCUSHION

The butterfly pincushion takes very little time to make and you can just use scrap felt pieces, so I'd suggest making one for each one of your "sewing" friends.

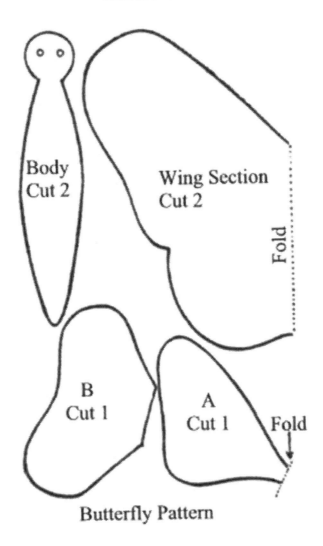

Butterfly Pattern

You can use any color felt scraps that you may have --- use any type of coordinating colors or contrasting colors that are handy. We've used green for the outer wings and yellow for the interior wings, and made solid green for the back.

Using the pattern pieces above as a guide, cut the number of each piece as indicated - two of the large wing section (one for the front and one for the back). Cut two body sections, then cut one each of A and B, using contrasting colors if desired.

Pin wing sections A and B to the top of the large wing section as illustrated, then using embroidery floss stitch an outline stitch all around wing sections A and B.

Next overcast the two body sections together, using thread to match the body color, and lightly stuff with cotton batting as you go. Before closing the opening at the head, make eyes with small stitches of yellow embroidery floss on the upper side. With six strands of the same yellow floss, take a few stitches on the underside of the body below the head; take a long, slant stitch across the upper side and around to the underneath again; again take a few stitches on the underneath and another long slant stitch across the upper side, continuing this way until you reach the bottom of the body.

Tack the finished body to the upper wing section. Overcast the front wing section to the back section, stuffing with cotton batting as you go.

When finished, you can attach a small plastic ring behind the head for hanging, as shown above, or you can leave it as it is so it can lay on the sewing table.

Learn How To Sew

HEART BOOKMARK

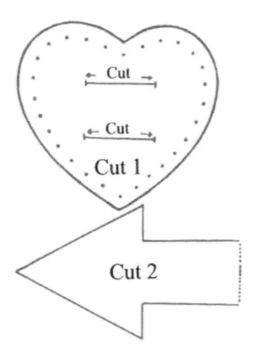

MATERIALS NEEDED:

2" Square of red felt

Strip of black felt 1 ½" x 12"

28 small white beads

1 red button – size of a nickel

Red embroidery floss

    Using the pattern above, cut the heart from the red felt square. Cut along the two "cut" lines as indicated. Sew the white beads around the edge of the heart, or try your skill with French Knots (see "hand sewing techniques" section) in place of the beads.
    From the black felt, cut 2 strips 12 inches long, shaping one end like an arrow, following the outline above. Place one on top of the other and with red embroidery floss overcast the edges around the arrow shaped end, and about one-half inch on the arrow shaft. Slip on piece of the black felt through the heart, then continue overcastting the edges. Sew the button at the opposite end.
    The following illustration shows what the finished bookmark will look like.

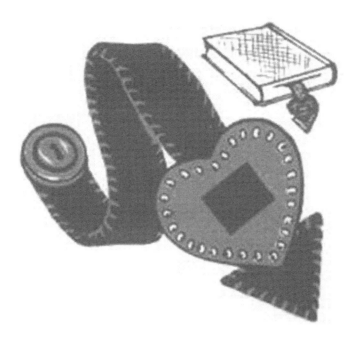

    The bookmarks are so easily made that you can give one to each of your friends that love to read.

    All of the hand sewing projects are the type that can be done while you're watching TV, or perhaps waiting at a doctor's office, etc. Simply put all your materials into a small zip lock bag, slip it into your purse and you're ready to go.

21 WHEN YOUR CHILD WANTS TO SEW

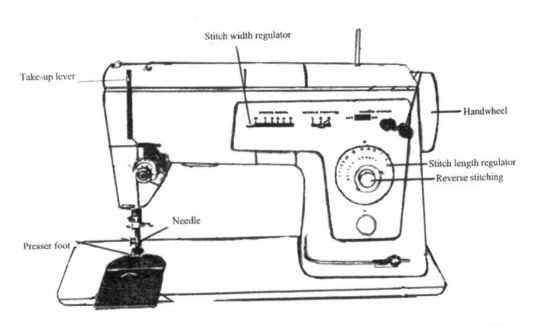

There will come a time when your children will want to learn how to sew. All children want to do what Mommy is doing, or what Daddy is doing, and it's a fantastic thing that they want to copy us and learn from us. As with teaching a child any new thing, there is a great deal of patience that goes into it.

Very small children should learn the basics of sewing via the hand sewing method – using sewing cards that are safe for small hands. Sewing cards we recommend can be found at the following website: (http://sewwithsarah.com/product-category/e-z-sew-sewing-cards/) - for 3-7 years old.

After the child has become proficient with the sewing cards and even perhaps a little older, they can graduate up to hand sewing doll clothes, small pillows, sewing on large buttons, etc., using a very large needle, loose woven fabric and heavy thread. NOTE: When the child graduates to using a "real" needle for handsewing, they must be very closely supervised to prevent injury to themselves or to another child.

As the child matures he/she will want to learn to use the sewing machine as well. You know your child better than we do to know the maturity of the child, and if the child shows the interest necessary to learn some sewing rules and be able to follow them.

To begin with, simply show the child the **basics** of sewing machine operation and where the sewing machine parts that he/she will be using (see the illustration on the previous page).

Teach the child how to straight stitch first, insuring that you teach them to keep both hands away from the needle area. The left hand guides the fabric only from the left side; the right guides the material from the right side only. Teach them to never put their hand or fingers in front of the needle area while the machine is running. (These things seem so petty to us because we've been sewing "forever", but to a beginner, it is extremely important to teach the safety items as well as how to make the stitches.)

After YOU feel comfortable that they can follow your instructions on the sewing procedure and safety procedures, you can move on to show them how to do zig-zag stitching, starting and stopping the sewing machine, removing the fabric from the needle area, and keeping their fingers out from under the needle. Don't get them confused by trying to show them how to take a needle out of the clamp, or how to rewind a bobbin, etc until after they've had considerable experience with just the basic sewing (you do the bobbin changing, needle changing, etc) and are ready to learn some new things. Keep in mind that you will need to supervise the child very closely with all operations of the sewing machine.

A suggestion that you might want to consider if your child shows a keen interest in sewing is to get them "their own" sewing machine – perhaps from a second hand store, or a yard sale. This would be good especially if you have one of the "top of the line" electronic sewing machines that you're really a little bit worried about letting small hands "play around" with it. A good used (and usually cheap) sewing machine on their sewing table would definitely be easier for you to monitor (you'd be close by on your own machine), and you'd be creating memories that will last a lifetime for the child as the two of you "sew" together.

Sewing machine care and maintenance will change a little after children start to use the machine. The following recommendations will make life a little easier for you if your child was the last one to use the machine.

1. Always wipe the machine down with a damp cloth – sometimes children may have sticky fingers, etc., and you don't want to start out with spots on your fabric before the garment is finished.
2. Always check the stitch length and width – you may be used to leaving it on a certain setting, which may have been changed while the child was sewing.
3. Clean the lint from the tension discs, throat plate area, and bobbin area at least monthly. Nothing will cause more problems than a build-up of lint and broken thread pieces.
4. Make a new cleaning and oiling schedule for the machine, especially if you do a lot of sewing, and now your son or daughter is also doing a lot of sewing.
5. Take out the needle and roll it on the sewing table to be certain it is not bent. Check the point on the needle to see that it isn't rough. If there's any question whether the needle is still good or not, replace it.
6. Check the size of the needle – your child may have been hemming a pair of jeans with a large heavy duty needle. Check for compatibility, don't risk damaging a new silk blouse!

Now that you've gotten some "hands on" experience with a sewing machine, as well as making items with the "sewing machine" projects as well as the "hand sewing" projects, we feel like you have a very good start on a life long hobby. We hope you will enjoy your sewing experiences, and that you will continue to expand your knowledge. Happy Sewing!

22 RECOMMENDED RESOURCES

http://SewWithSarah.com ~ Your pattern and pattern making headquarters!

http://PlusSizeChildren.com ~ Patterns, classes, books and links that make it easier to sew for plus size children!

http://PatternsThatFitYou.com ~ The online fashion design school teaches the art of custom fitting patterns and pattern making to beginners and experts alike.

http://Patterns2Go.com ~ A variety of patterns to choose from – sewing, crafting, knitting, crochet, tatting, and more.

http://SewMachineRepair.com ~ Learn how to repair your own treadle, serger and sewing machines and save yourself time, money and frustration.

http://101WaysToTieAScarf.com ~ Scarves, the versatile accessory! Learn how to make scarves and 101 ways to tie them.

http://SewWithLeather.com ~ Everything you need to know about sewing with leather.

http://CouponClutch.com ~ Carry your coupons in one of these fashionable fabric covered 3 ring binders.

http://WomInfo.com ~ The go-to site for women in business, or who want to be in business.

http://ShopperStrategy.com ~ Be a better shopper! Tips and reviews from a frugal shopper.

http://SewingBusiness.com ~ Information plus tutorials for those who sew and for those in the business of sewing for others.

http://youcanworkathomenow.com/ ~ Work at home tutorials – helping you make money online!

23 PRACTICE PAGES

Learn How To Sew

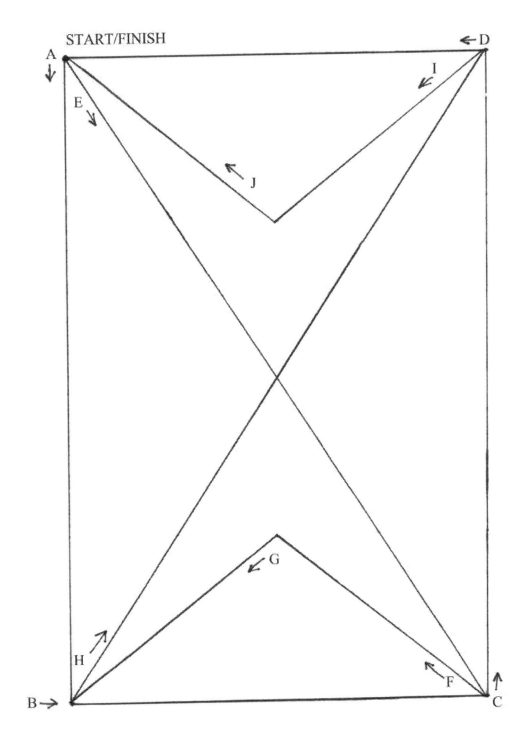

81

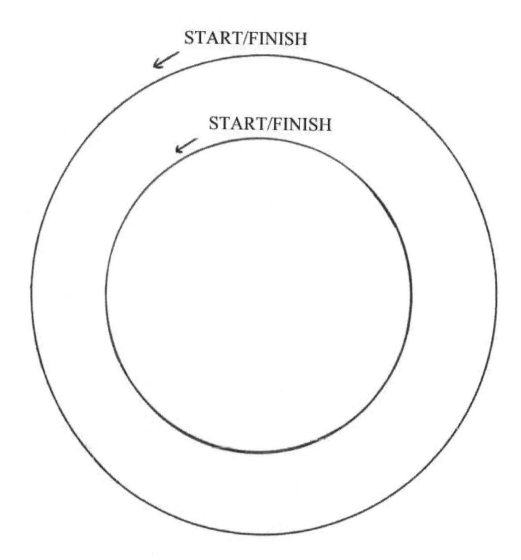

Learn How To Sew

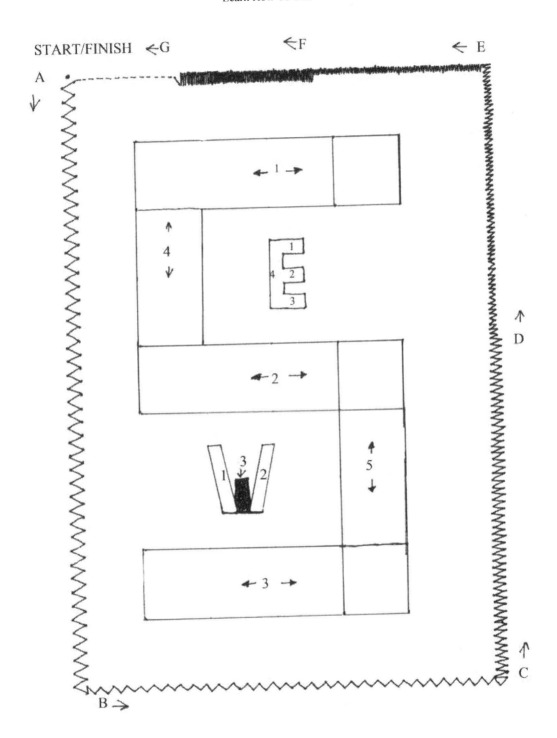

ABOUT THE AUTHOR

Sarah Doyle learned to sew at the age of 8 on her mother's treadle Sewing machine, and found a lifelong passion.

Sarah officially started her sewing and pattern making career in 1970 with a military assignment to Taiwan. She had been taking in sewing and alterations to help make ends meet for their family of 6 children, when her husband received orders for Taiwan. She was excited about the prospect of being able to learn something about Oriental pattern making because it would give her a chance to "make patterns that would fit my customers perfectly".

Sarah attended a yearlong pattern making class at a local Taiwanese school with the help of an English speaking Taiwanese lady, then she began writing her first book, "Sarah's Key To Pattern Drafting".

After returning to the U.S., Sarah started teaching pattern drafting classes to the general public as well as "for credit" classes for home economics teachers. She then made the classes available by mail order so those who could not attend her classes would also have the opportunity to learn pattern making.

With the internet explosion, a fast paced society, and so little time for organized classes, Sarah once again filled a real need for the sewers around the world by painstakingly setting up and making available online every class, book and pattern she had authored.

Starting with just one book "Sarah's Key to Pattern Drafting" and a long list of people wanting that book in 1976, Sarah now has over 35 sewing, pattern making, pattern make-over, craft, quilting, embroidery, sewing machine repair and general how-to books available, in addition to a line of clothing patterns for plus size children.

After retiring from the U.S. Air Force, Sarah's husband, Reuben, started doing sewing machine repair as a sideline business. After many years of sewing machine repair, his family talked him into putting his information into book form so he would be able to help those in need of sewing machine repair but lived too far away for him to go fix the machine.

Reuben and Sarah decided to combine their talents to write this book on learning how to sew.

Made in the USA
Lexington, KY
12 September 2017